12 MARINE ANIMALS
BACK FROM THE BRINK

by Nancy Furstinger

www.12StoryLibrary.com

12-Story Library is an imprint of Peterson Publishing Company and Press Room Editions.

Produced for 12-Story Library by Red Line Editorial

Photographs ©: Shane Myers Photography/Shutterstock Images, cover, 1, 5, 28; Mavrick/ Shutterstock Images, 4; worldwildlifewonders/Shutterstock Images, 6; Terence/Shutterstock Images, 7; A Cotton Photo/Shutterstock Images, 8; Kipling Brock/Shutterstock Images, 9; creativex/Shutterstock Images, 10; FiledImage/Shutterstock Images, 11; Stephen Meese/ Shutterstock Images, 12; John_Lancaster/Thinkstock, 13; NancyS/Shutterstock Images, 14; birdiegal/Shutterstock Images, 15, 29; Micha Klootwijk/Shutterstock Images, 16; Menno Schaefer/Shutterstock Images, 17; Jo Crebin/Shutterstock Images, 18; James Michael Dorsey/Shutterstock Images, 19; Travis Cooper/Thinkstock, 20; Joe Belanger/Shutterstock Images, 21; idreamphoto/Shutterstock Images, 22; Joost van Uffelen/Shutterstock Images, 23; US Fish and Wildlife/AP Images, 24; Liz Labunski/US Fish and Wildlife/AP Images, 25; ayzek/Shutterstock Images, 26; Nickolay Stanev/Shutterstock Images, 27

ISBN
978-1-63235-004-6 (hardcover)
978-1-63235-064-0 (paperback)
978-1-62143-045-2 (hosted ebook)

Library of Congress Control Number: 2014937259

Printed in the United States of America
Mankato, MN
June, 2014

Go beyond the book. Get free, up-to-date content on this topic at 12StoryLibrary.com.

TABLE OF CONTENTS

GREEN SEA TURTLES NEARLY VANISH OFF THE HAWAIIAN ISLANDS

Green sea turtles have been on Earth for 245 million years. That means they have been around since before the dinosaurs became extinct. They are one of the largest sea turtle species in the world. These sturdy animals can live more than 80 years in the wild. But over-hunting almost killed them all.

For decades, Hawaiians liked to hunt the sea turtles. People ate steaks made of their meat. They stirred their fat into soups and turned their skin into gloves.

As hunters were catching more and more sea turtles, scientists became concerned. Green sea turtles reproduce slowly. They only visit the nesting grounds once every three to

Green sea turtles come ashore to lay eggs.

IUCN RED LIST

The International Union for the Conservation of Nature (IUCN) keeps a list of all threatened species in the world, called the Red List. Each species is labeled according to how at risk it is.

Least Concern: Not considered at risk.
Near Threatened: At risk of being vulnerable or endangered in the future.
Vulnerable: At risk of extinction.
Endangered: At high risk of extinction.
Critically Endangered: At extremely high risk of extinction.
Extinct in the Wild: Only lives in captivity.
Extinct: No members of a species are left.

500

Maximum weight in pounds (227 kg) of a green sea turtle.

Status: Least concern
Population: 800 nesting females in Hawaii
Home: Hawaii
Life Span: 60–70 years

The US Fish and Wildlife Service sprang into action. It listed the species as threatened. It became illegal to kill green sea turtles.

The turtles started to make a slow comeback. The population has been increasing for 25 years. In recent years, more than 800 females have nested on the Hawaiian Islands.

four years. One concerned scientist decided to start tracking them. In 1973, he counted just 67 nesting females. Not enough turtles were hatching to make up for those being hunted. If hunting continued, the green sea turtles would be gone from Hawaii.

Sea turtles stay warm by swimming close to the surface of the water.

SOUTHERN SEA OTTER MAKES A SURPRISE COMEBACK

Sea otters spend most of their time in water. When they're not swimming or fishing, they float on their backs. They wrap their bodies in sea plants. This keeps them from drifting away while resting. The otters' thick fur keeps them warm in the cold water.

Sea otters' fur is very soft. It repels water well, too. The warm coats people made out of sea otter fur used to be very popular. So many people wanted these coats that hunters killed many sea otters. The sea otters were close to becoming extinct.

As many as 16,000 southern sea otters used to live in California. It appeared they were all gone by the early 1900s. For a while, people thought there were no southern sea otters left in California. They were surprised to find approximately 50 southern sea otters there in 1938.

By then, hunting sea otters had been banned. Southern sea otter numbers in California climbed to more than 3,000.

After eating, sea otters wash themselves in sea water.

25

Percent of its body weight a southern sea otter must eat every day to make up for the energy it burns to keep warm.

Status: Endangered
Population:
    Approximately 3,000
Home: California
Life Span: 10–20 years

STAYING WARM

Sea otters have up to 1 million hairs per square inch (6.45 sq cm). Compare that to the 100,000 hairs on your entire head! They also keep warm by tumbling in water. This traps air bubbles in their fur. The bubbles help keep in warmth.

Sea otters eat clams. They use rocks to break open the shells.

GRACEFUL "SEA COWS" FIND A SAFE HOME

Florida manatees are large mammals that swim in waters off the state's coast. They are sometimes called "sea cows" because they eat plants, just as cows eat grass. They swim in short bursts and rise to breathe air. These animals have no enemies in nature. But people have put them at risk.

Manatees never leave the water.

Speed limits for boats help protect manatees.

MANATEE ZONE
SLOW SPEED
MINIMUM WAKE
OCT 1 THRU APRIL 30
25 MPH
REMAINDER OF YEAR
PERMIT NO. 92-037   68C22.011   11 FAC

Manatees swim slowly. This made them easy targets for hunting. Hunters turned their hides into clothing. They used their fat for oil. By the mid-1900s, the manatees' numbers were dropping fast.

15

A manatee's top speed in miles per hour (24 km/h).

Status: Endangered
Home: Coastal waters of Florida
Population: More than 4,500
Life Span: 40 years

New laws banning hunting helped manatees make a turnaround. The 1972 Marine Mammal Protection Act now protects them. So does the Endangered Species Act. But manatees still face other threats. Speeding boats sometimes injure them. Many manatees have scars from boat propellers.

In 1978, Florida became a safer place for sea cows. The state posted speed limits for boats. It started fining speeders. Boats were banned from some spots where manatees swim. These changes have helped the population rise to more than 4,500.

9

GIANT "SEA ELEPHANTS" BEAT THE ODDS

Elephant seals are the largest of all seals. Males can top the scales at 4,400 pounds (2,000 kg). These seals can puff up their snouts so they look like trunks. That's how they earned the nickname "sea elephant." But one kind of elephant seal, the northern, almost vanished from the Pacific Ocean.

Thousands of elephant seals once bred on the beaches of the West Coast. The seals had something hunters wanted: blubber. This oily

Elephant seals come up on the beach during summer to molt, when they lose their fur and grow a new coat.

Male elephant seals sometimes fight with each other over mates.

fat stores energy. It helps seals stay alive in breeding season when they can't search for food.

People began hunting elephant seals in large numbers in the 1800s. Hunters waited for the seals to reach land. Then they shot them.

2

Hours an elephant seal can stay underwater without breathing.

Status: Least concern
Population: 171,000
Home: North Pacific Ocean
Life Span: Nine years

They boiled the seals' blubber to make oil. The oil was used to light lamps and grease machines.

Elephant seals spend nine months of the year at sea. So hunters were never able to kill the entire population at once. But by the late 1800s, only approximately 20 elephant seals could be found. They were close to becoming extinct.

Both the Mexican and US governments banned hunting of elephant seals in the early 1900s. Since then, their numbers have risen to an estimated 171,000. Scientists think this number is close to what it was before the seals were hunted.

RIGHT WHALE NUMBERS STOP HEADING THE WRONG WAY

North Atlantic right whales chug slowly through the water. They weigh up to 70 tons (63.5 metric tons). That's around the same size as 10 African elephants. Their heads make up one-fourth of their 50-foot (15-m) length. Their size and slow speed make them easy for hunters to spot.

These whales got their name because they were said to be the "right" ones to hunt. They were easy to catch. Plus their thick blubber causes them to float after being killed. Whalers could then tow them to shore.

Whalers hunted right whales for hundreds of years. Only a few dozen were left in the North Atlantic by 1935. That year, hunting was banned. The population started to

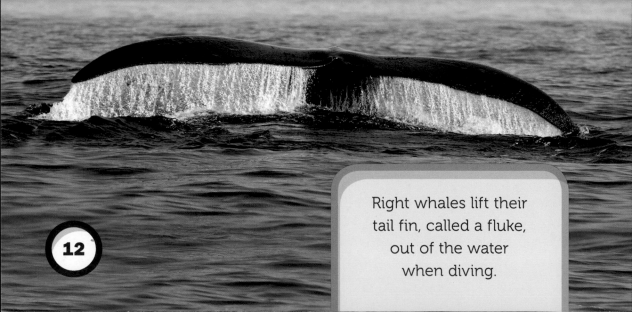

Right whales lift their tail fin, called a fluke, out of the water when diving.

Right whales can swim underwater for up to 20 minutes before coming up to the surface for air.

grow slowly. But adult females give birth to only one calf every three to five years. At this rate, it takes many years for the number to grow.

By the 1990s, only 300 right whales were swimming in the North Atlantic. Scientists thought too many ships were crashing into whales. Some ships' routes were changed. By 2013, the number of right whales had risen to 500. This was the most right whales in hundreds of years.

STRAINED FOOD

Right whales have approximately 250 pairs of "teeth" called baleen. Baleen is made of keratin, like hair. It grows up to 9.5 feet (2.9 m) long! Whales use it to strain food as they swim. They can gobble 125 pounds (57 kg) of krill and small fish per hour.

15
Length in feet (5 m) of a right whale calf at birth.

Status: Endangered
Population:
Approximately 500
Home: North Atlantic Ocean
Life Span: 50 years

EASTERN STELLER SEA LIONS TAKEN OFF THE ENDANGERED LIST

Eastern Steller sea lions are noisy. During breeding season, large numbers charge onto beaches. The males fight over areas of land. Some of their pups are even crushed by the crowd. At other times, they hunt for fish, squid, and octopus in the Pacific Ocean.

People started hunting Steller sea lions in the 1800s. They used their meat, blubber, and skins. They even turned their whiskers into pipe cleaners. Later people killed the sea lions for another reason.

Steller sea lions follow fishing boats. They eat the same kinds of fish that people try to catch. Some fishers started shooting the sea lions so that they would stop taking so many fish.

Steller sea lions often swim great distances to find food.

2,500

Weight in pounds (1,134 kg) of an Eastern Steller sea lion.

Status: Unlisted
Population: Approximately 70,000
Home: North Pacific Ocean
Life Span: 20–30 years

THINK ABOUT IT

How do you think fishers could keep sea lions from following their boats? Should both have the same right to catch fish?

In the 1950s, approximately 300,000 Steller sea lions were in the Pacific Ocean. By the late 1970s, there were only 18,000. They were listed as endangered in 1990. Fishers had to stop shooting them.

Their numbers climbed back up to 70,000 by 2010. Three years later, they were taken off the US endangered list. But it is still illegal to harm them.

Steller sea lions growl and roar loudly when they gather on beaches.

7

GRAY SEALS SPLASH BACK INTO ACTION

Off the coast of New England, gray seals bob in the water. Their big eyes help them to spot a meal. Their sharp ears help them to zero in on prey. Then they grab fish using the claws on their flippers. But some fishers thought that the seals were eating too many cod. They wanted the animal gone.

In the late 1800s, Maine and Massachusetts started paying people to kill gray seals. The hunt ended in 1962. By then, approximately 135,000 seals had been killed. In 1972, the Marine Mammal Protection Act made sure gray seals were safe.

Gray seals have a thick layer of blubber to keep warm and help them float.

When a seal leaves the water for dry land, it is called "hauling out."

Since then, their numbers have been rising. On one island off Cape Cod, only five seal pups were born in 1988. By 2008, the island saw more than 2,000 born. Now they star on seal cams.

People watch live videos of seals on Maine's Seal Island!

100
Pounds (45 kg) a gray seal pup gains in its first three weeks.

Status: Least concern
Population: 7,300 in US waters
Home: North Atlantic Ocean
Life Span: 25–35 years

DEADLY JAWS

Seals draw great white sharks to Cape Cod. Tour boats take people to see sharks that come to eat the seals. People put special tags on 34 great whites so satellites could track them. They found out the same sharks return each summer. The sharks know that an easy meal waits for them.

GRAY WHALES ONCE AGAIN RULE THE SEA

Gray whales log up to 14,000 miles (22,530 km) when they migrate each year. They leave their summer feeding grounds in the Bering Sea. They travel south to Mexico in the winter. The whales mate and give birth to calves in lagoons. These used to be secret spots. But then people found their hiding places.

After giving birth, gray whales stay in the lagoons while their calves grow.

After three months, the calves have built up enough blubber for their trip north. But in the 1850s, whalers found the lagoons. They began hunting the whale calves.

Whalers called mother whales "devil fish." The whales sometimes smashed boats to shield their calves. The mothers were unable to

Gray whales have two blowholes. They can spray water up to 15 feet (5 m).

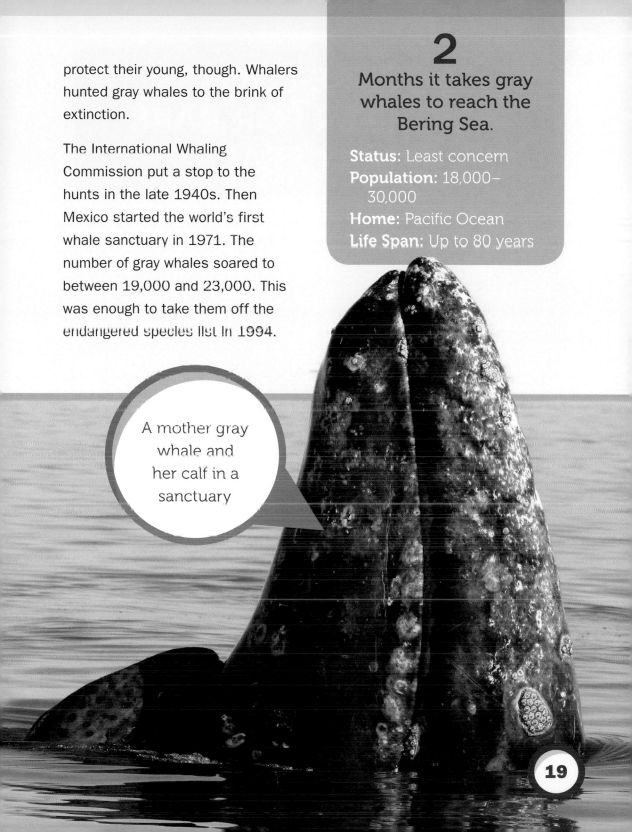

protect their young, though. Whalers hunted gray whales to the brink of extinction.

The International Whaling Commission put a stop to the hunts in the late 1940s. Then Mexico started the world's first whale sanctuary in 1971. The number of gray whales soared to between 19,000 and 23,000. This was enough to take them off the endangered species list in 1994.

2
Months it takes gray whales to reach the Bering Sea.

Status: Least concern
Population: 18,000–30,000
Home: Pacific Ocean
Life Span: Up to 80 years

A mother gray whale and her calf in a sanctuary

FUTURE LOOKS BRIGHTER FOR RARE FURRY SEALS

Guadalupe fur seals breed on only one island off of Mexico. The island is tropical. So the seals go for long swims during the day to stay cool. They have strong front flippers that let them speed across sand and water. Because they live in one small area of the world, not much is known about the seals. For many years, scientists even thought they might be extinct.

Guadalupe fur seals are the rarest of all fur seal species.

The government of Mexico has made Guadalupe Island a sanctuary for fur seals and other marine species.

In the 1700s and 1800s, people hunted them for their thick fur. By the early 1900s, Guadalupe fur seals seemed to be gone. But then scientists found a few dozen left on Guadalupe Island in 1928. They took two to the San Diego Zoo to study them.

In 1975, Mexico turned the seals' island home into a sanctuary. Now between 15,000 and 17,000 fur seals breed there.

33
Percent of Guadalupe fur seal pups that died in storms and hurricanes in 1992.

Status: Near threatened
Population: 15,000–17,000
Home: Guadalupe Island, Mexico
Life Span: 20 years

THINK ABOUT IT

If you were a scientist, what questions would you have about fur seals? What might be good ways to learn more about them?

HUMPBACK WHALES ARE STILL SINGING

People go on whale-watching cruises to see humpback whales. Humpbacks can often be seen leaping out of the water. Then all 40 tons (36 t) of the whale comes crashing back down. This is called breaching. Sometimes a humpback will lift the top third of its body out of the water to look around. This is called spyhopping. Other times the humpback will slap its tail against the ocean repeatedly.

This tail is called a fluke. No two flukes are colored or shaped the same. Scientists are able to track and count humpback whales by their flukes. That's how scientists knew the whales' numbers had fallen too low half a century ago.

When a whale leaps out of the water, it is called breaching.

Humpback whales migrate between feeding grounds and breeding grounds each year.

Before the 1900s, an estimated 100,000 humpback whales swam in the Pacific and Atlantic Oceans. But whalers hunted them by the thousands. By 1966, only approximately 1,400 remained.

That was when the International Whaling Commission banned the hunting of humpbacks. Afterward, the population started rising again. Approximately 55,000 humpback whales now swim in the Pacific and Atlantic Oceans.

MALE CHOIR

Only male humpback whales sing. They sing patterns. Each one repeats. All males in each region sing the same songs. They can sing for hours at a time. Their songs can be heard up to 20 miles (30 km) away. Scientists believe they sing to find mates.

10
Age at which a humpback whale is fully grown.

Status: Least concern
Population: Approximately 55,000
Home: North Pacific Ocean, North Atlantic Ocean
Life Span: 50 years

PROTECTED PACIFIC WALRUSES HAUL OUT ON SEA ICE

Walruses use their big tusks like tools. Pacific walruses also use their tusks to pull themselves up onto sheets of sea ice. Their tusks also act as drills. They can make breathing holes in ice. And the tusks act as swords when males battle for mates. But people also wanted Pacific walruses' tusks.

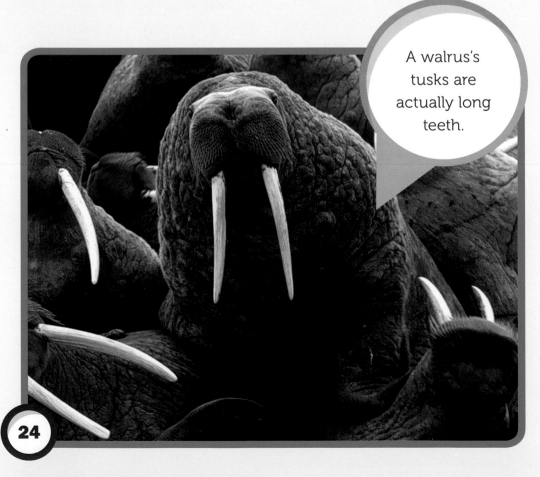

A walrus's tusks are actually long teeth.

CLIMATE CHANGE

Walruses face a new threat from climate change. Warmer temperatures have caused sea ice to shrink. Mother walruses must swim far to find food. They leave their babies unprotected for longer amounts of time. When the mothers return, they have less room on the ice for breeding and caring for their families.

Hunters used to shoot walruses for their ivory tusks. Artists carved them and sold them. People also ate walrus meat. They used walrus oil for lamps. The Congressional Walrus Act banned hunting in 1941. Protected from hunters, walrus numbers started to rise. By 1990, there were more than 200,000 Pacific walruses.

24
Ice thickness in inches (61 cm) needed to support a walrus's weight.

Status: Unlisted
Population: More than 200,000 in 1990
Home: Pacific Ocean
Life Span: Up to 40 years

When Pacific walruses aren't swimming, they haul out on sea ice or on the shore.

WATERS SAFER NOW FOR PLAYFUL HECTOR'S DOLPHINS

The Hector's dolphin is a rare dolphin that lives in New Zealand. People love to watch these dolphins. It often looks like they are playing and doing tricks. They leap into the air. They lift their bodies up out of the water and turn around. Sometimes they blow bubbles or play with seaweed. But they can get tangled in fishing nets when they are playing or searching for food.

Like other mammals living in the ocean, Hector's dolphins need to come up to the surface to breathe. If they are stuck in a net underwater, they will drown. New Zealand started a sanctuary in 1988. Hector's dolphins are now sheltered in the bays of New Zealand's Banks Peninsula.

Fishing nets are banned in some New Zealand coastal waters because of the danger to dolphins.

Hector's dolphins are one of the smallest dolphin species in the world.

Scientists track the dolphins with tags. They find out where they swim. Then boaters can stay away from these spots. Fishers also use alarms on their gear. The alarm makes a pinging sound. Dolphins are quick learners. They know that the alarm is a warning to stay away from nets. With fewer threats, Hector's dolphins are slowly on the rise. As of 2013, they numbered more than 7,000.

4

Number of calves a typical female Hector's dolphin will have in a lifetime.

Status: Endangered
Population: More than 7,000
Home: New Zealand
Life Span: 20 years

THINK ABOUT IT

How else could technology be used to protect dolphins or other threatened species in the ocean?

FACT SHEET

- Many countries have laws protecting endangered animals. In 1973, the US Congress passed the Endangered Species Act. It requires state and federal government agencies to monitor and protect species that might become extinct. It also bans people from hunting, catching, trading, or possessing animals and plants that are protected.

- The two US federal agencies that deal with endangered species are the US Fish and Wildlife Service and the National Oceanic and Atmospheric Administration. Both have departments dedicated to identifying and helping endangered species.

- President Richard Nixon signed the Marine Mammals Protection Act in 1972. This act makes it illegal to hunt any marine mammal in US waters.

- Scientists use different methods for tracking a species. They can tell manatees apart by the unique scars they receive in collisions with boat propellers. Scientists photograph each scar and enter it in a computer catalog. Researchers can spot individual right whales by the pattern of white patches on their big heads. Sometimes scientists will attach a tag to an animal for tracking.

- When Congress created the Endangered Species List in 1966, the Guadalupe fur seal was listed. Two other marine animals appeared on the first list: the Caribbean monk seal and the Florida manatee.

- Oil spills can be dangerous to marine animals. Crude oil can coat an animal's or bird's fur or feathers. Oil affects animals' ability to stay warm and keeps them from moving normally. It can also be poisonous if swallowed. Oil on the ocean's surface can lower the oxygen levels below.

- Forty countries belong to the International Whaling Commission. This organization governs whaling practices worldwide. It also encourages research and sets aside protected areas for whales.

GLOSSARY

baleen
A substance that hangs down from the upper jaw of certain whales.

blubber
The fat of large sea mammals, such as whales.

breeding
The process by which animals or plants are produced by their parents.

endangered
Threatened with extinction.

extinct
The death of all members of a species.

flipper
A broad, flat limb used for swimming.

fluke
The end of a whale's tail, used to help it move through water.

krill
Small shrimp-like creatures in the ocean.

lagoon
A shallow channel connected to a larger body of water.

migrate
To pass from one region to another on a regular schedule for feeding or breeding.

sanctuary
A place where a wildlife species is protected.

threatened
To be in danger of becoming extinct.

FOR MORE INFORMATION

Books

Christopherson, Sara Cohen. *Top 50 Reasons to Care about Whales and Dolphins: Animals in Peril.* Berkeley Heights, NJ: Enslow Publishers, 2010.

Marsh, Laura. *National Geographic Readers: Manatees.* Washington, DC: National Geographic Children's Books, 2014.

Pringle, Laurence. *Whales! Strange and Wonderful.* Honesdale, PA: Boyds Mills Press, 2012.

Quirk, Joe. *Call to the Rescue: The Story of the Marine Mammal Center.* San Francisco: Chronicle Books, 2009.

Websites

Dolphin Research Center: Kids Marine Animal Station
www.dolphins.org/kids_marine_animal_station

Kids Do Ecology: Marine Mammals
kids.nceas.ucsb.edu/mmp

The Marine Mammal Center
www.marinemammalcenter.org/education/teacher-resources

National Geographic Kids: The Ocean
kids.nationalgeographic.com/kids/activities/new/ocean

INDEX

About the Author
Nancy Furstinger is the author of almost 100 books, including many on animals. She has been a feature writer for a daily newspaper, a managing editor of trade and consumer magazines, and an editor at two children's book publishing houses.

READ MORE FROM 12-STORY LIBRARY

Every 12-Story Library book is available in many formats, including Amazon Kindle and Apple iBooks. For more information, visit your device's store or 12StoryLibrary.com.